I'm Ollie Flintlock,

Nice to Meet You!

TANYA GREEN

DEDICATION

To Nana – Jordan's going to be just fine. ☺

TABLE OF CONTENTS

ACKNOWLEDGMENTS

Giving thanks to my in house children:
Taliyah, Justin and Jordan; you make being a
mom more fun and rewarding every day.
And to my adult daughter, Tanesha, I love
you today just
as much as I did the day you entered my life.
I am blessed to have been gifted with each
and every one of you.

1
THE BEGINNING

Ok, first let me set the record straight. The picture on the cover of this book **is** me, but I'm not eleven there. I mean, look at those **little** glasses on that **little** face. Does that look like an eleven year old to you? In **that** picture I'm only 7. I told my mom we should put the picture I took last month on the cover. It was a picture of me at my favorite pizza place. But she thought this one would be better for my story. So - there it is!

Oh, by the way I'm Ollie - Ollie Flintlock. Nice to meet you. If you have some time, I'd like to tell you a bit about myself. My mom always tells me that if I hope to learn anything about someone or something, I should be willing to offer a little about myself. You know, put in a little work. So, here I go. But I'm going to try my absolute hardest to put in a bit **more** than a little work, because I really want us to get to know each other.

Where should I start – let me see? Hey, I know! How about at the beginning, the day I entered this brave new world!? Funny, I believe I heard those words together somewhere before. I'm pretty sure that's the name of a book. Oh, by the way, I love books. For Christmas last year I got seven new books - best Christmas ever! Ok, so back to the beginning. It's strange to me that it is MY beginning, yet I don't actually remember it. I have heard a LOT about it though. So I'm going to be able to tell you about it from all of the things that I've heard about it.

The day was February 3 of the year 2002.

This country, The United States of America, was preparing to watch Mariah Carey sing the national anthem during the halftime show of the New England Patriots at the St. Louis Rams (Super Bowl XXXVI). I don't know why they name the Super Bowls with Roman numerals. Afterall, this isn't Italy! However, at some point somebody started naming them that way and it just kept going from there I suppose. So Roman numerals for the Super Bowls it is. Besides this isn't France either, and yet we have French Fries and French toast. Thank goodness for that! So, I guess Roman numeral Super Bowl labels are just fine after all.

As for me, well, on that day, I was officially making my entrance into this world. The doctor was getting me out of my mom's stomach and she and my dad were busy being the happiest they could ever remember being. At least, that's what they've told me. I've thought about this a lot though and I believe they might have told my brother and sisters the same thing. Sooooo!?

But still, yes, this was a great day for us all. Really, I'm quite positive it was. Seriously, it had to be the greatest day ever for me! With all of the hanging around in my mom's stomach for almost a year with no internet, video games, or TV, how did I ever survive in there!? It sounds like jail for babies if you ask me. That's what makes me sure that February 3rd of the year 2002 was the greatest day ever and that I was super happy to be born!

Only two days later another great thing happened, my mom and dad took me out of the hospital. I was headed for the place my parents and my sister Tayasia called home. I bet they kept saying things like, "We're going home now Ollie" and "You're going to love your room son".

Now as I just said in the last paragraph, my sister's name is Tayasia. She's my oldest sister. I have a younger sister too. You'll hear a little more about her later in the story. Long before I was born a decision was made to call Tayasia, Aysia. Yet another thing I don't quite understand like the Superbowl's Roman numerals thing. My name's Ollie, but they don't call me Oll, Lie or Lee. Do you see why I'm confused? Why would parents go through all of the trouble of coming up with what their child's name will be, only to call them something else later? So strange adults are! Anyway, she'd been the star of the house for the past six years, and now she was going to teach me all about how to be a star too. After all, it was her job, a sort of big sister law or something like that.

As for me being born, I think she might have been just as happy as mom and dad. She was always smiling at me. She smiled even more than they did! And the talking, whoa, she really did a lot of that! Apparently, she talked to me about absolutely everything. There were talks about school; talks about cooking; and many talks about SpongeBob®. Oh she really loved SpongeBob®. Although, I think maybe I was her best friend back then. She loved me so much!

2
ORDINARY CLUMSINESS?

Eventually I learned to crawl, walk and even talk. Things were changing. Soon I was even running. Now it was Aysia who had to listen to **me** talk about everything and I'm sure sometimes she wished we were back at the day when I was just born again.

I got older fast, and for my second birthday, which I actually remember, I got a big shiny red firetruck. I pushed it and rode on it all over the house. I loved it so much! It's a great thing that somebody realized little boys would like toy firetrucks, because they were so awesome. Mom and dad saw how happy the firetruck made me so they bought me more and more trucks. I soon had more kinds of trucks than probably any other little boy in my town. After a while I started liking cars too. I had so many of both of them that they fell out of my closet every time I opened the door.

One day I was doing a turbo jump from the sofa to the coffee table, with one of my super-fast cars. The table was pretty close, but somehow I still missed the jump. My face hit the table really - really – really – really hard. In a flash, my mouth filled up with something warm that tasted like 20 nickels, that's a dollar by the way. My mom came running and screaming "My goodness son. What did you do to your mouth? I don't know why you're so clumsy lately! I don't think this is ordinary".

Where did she come from so fast? How did she know what happened? Did she hear the crash? Did my mouth make a loud noise? I didn't know the answer to any of those questions, but I'm sure glad she was there, because as soon as she got there my mouth started hurting super awful and the warm liquid in it was no longer staying there. It was now pouring down my chin and dripping all over the floor. Turns out this liquid was blood. I had never seen blood in real life before and had no idea so much of it could come from inside of my skin walls by itself. I thought a doctor had to use a needle to go way under your skin for blood to get out.

My mom had said that I was being **super** clumsy lately. Which means that I must have already been some kind of regular clumsy. And I don't know what kind of clumsy it was then, but this clumsy was definitely no fun at all and I sure hope it wasn't going to continue.

Many months passed and my mouth had

been back to normal a long time ago. But I somehow couldn't stop thinking about that day. It was like I was stuck there. I don't know why, but that was the day my super thinking started. How had my legs make the big mistake of not getting me to the table? What did my mom mean when she said this clumsy wasn't ordinary? How many times before had ordinary clumsy happened to me?

And I wasn't just having super thinking about the memories of my mouth accident. I was thinking hard about lots of other things too. My mind had somehow turned into a super thinking machine and I was in deep thought about everything all the time.

Sadly, the word clumsy quickly became a regular part of my life. I was doing things such as walking into the side of open doors, wasting whole cups of liquids even though they had tops on them, and tripping over air or even my own feet. I thought sometimes this new clumsy of mine was making my mom really sad. One time I heard her tell someone, "I really don't think this is ordinary clumsiness"!

And she was right, I'd seen other kids in daycare and on tv, and it didn't look like any kids my age were having my same kind of clumsy. But as much as I was being clumsy, that wasn't my biggest problem. The real problem was this new super thinking machine that my brain had turn into. It was helping the clumsy stay around and I couldn't seem to turn it off. If I was sitting while super thinking, I was fine. But if I was moving while super thinking **then** the trouble came, because that's when most of the clumsy would happen. The super thinking machine kept me inside of my head all the time, so my legs didn't always know which direction to take me because my brain wasn't talking to them. They were just moving by themselves.

Other parts of me didn't always do what I wanted them to do either – like my hands and apparently lots of times my face. But I'd been watching my uncle Kahrel a lot and I didn't see it happening to him, EVER. Oh yea, you don't know who he is. My uncle Kahrel lived with us too back then. He's my mom's little brother, but he was like my BIG brother. He was super amazing at video games and I'm guessing he never had a problem with his hands doing what he told them to do. I think super clumsy just belonged to me.

I sure hope my little brother doesn't get clumsy or has the super thinking machine turn on in his brain one day like me. What!? Oh that's right, you didn't know I had a little brother either. Well, his name is Oscar. He's nine years old now. But during this time he was around 2 and he seemed to like me a lot, but I wasn't ever sure what to do with him or say to him so my mom rarely left us alone.

3
MY FRIEND, KING

Now if you were hoping I had more to say about Oscar or Kahrel here, sorry, maybe later. The year was now 2008 and big changes were happening almost every day. I had started elementary school. My Nana, the best grandmother ever, had gone to heaven. And I still miss not having her around. She used to take me to eat pizza every time I went to her house and she loved me so much. I now had a little sister, Talayla (Layla). And Kahrel? Well, he became an adult and decided to go into the Army. Why? I have no idea.

By now, I had become really good at playing all of the video games he played. Turns out video games were the one thing that turned the thinking machine into a thinking, reading, talking, exploring machine. With video games, the clumsy did not exist.

Before Kahrel left he gave me his Nintendo Game Cube®. I COULD NOT BELIEVE that it now belonged to me! I played the Sonic® game on it so much that one day it quit working and never started back. That made me so sad. But my mom had already bought me lots of other games and it was time that I started playing them. And I am so glad I did. Turned out, my thinking, reading, talking, exploring machine made me a super video game player. Even more super than Kahrel!

~

Soon I was in first grade. And as a first grader, you have to go to school for the whole day. That meant I couldn't play video games all the time anymore, even though I really wanted to. When I was able to play them though, I didn't really have anyone to play them with since Kahrel was gone. Dad was working a lot. Mom was taking care of my baby sister or working on her computer. Aysia was now 12 and spending most of her time doing schoolwork and girl stuff. And Oscar? Well he was big enough to follow me around and was going everywhere I went and trying to do everything I did. But he just wasn't big enough to talk to about video games or play them with like Kahrel.

The best chance I had of anybody playing games with me would have been mom. But one major thing was getting in the way of that - we now lived in the town where my mom was raised so people were always coming around to visit and talk to her. Most of the time they DIDN'T EVEN CALL FIRST, so we could never plan to do ANYTHING. It wasn't all bad though, because it stopped her from being so sad about my Nana going to heaven. Matter of fact I think the only reason we moved there is because of my mom's sadness over my Nana going to Heaven. Before we moved there, she used to go in the bathroom a lot to cry. I don't think she knew I could hear her though.

Getting away from sad stuff – I told you we were living in the town my mom was raised in, and I told you people were always coming by. But what I didn't tell you is just how many people. We had over a thousand family members there! And luckily for me, we moved into a house right across the street from one of the most awesome, nicest, kids I'd ever met. His name was

King and he became my best friend.

I'm sure you'd like to know how that happened – so here goes. Let me start off by telling you the most surprising part, I didn't have to figure out how to make him my friend. I actually didn't do much of anything at all.

I was in my room playing a video game when my mom told me someone was at the door looking for me. No one had ever been at the door for me, so I was most definitely confused, yet excited and even a bit scared all at the same time. Of course I knew my mom would never send me to the door to talk to a stranger, but that surely didn't stop me from feeling strange. This was definitely new to me.

I got to the door and it was King. "Hi Ollie"! he said. "I'm your cousin who lives across the street, whom your mom told you about. Would you like to come over to my house"? Many thoughts filled the thinking machine. "Go over to someone else's house? Why would I do that? All of my things are here in my house. What would I do over there? He would expect me to talk to him. People like to talk. I don't do that too much anymore since my thinking machine turned on. What would we talk about?" My super thinking got interrupted by King saying, "We can play some video games. I'll teach you if you don't know how". HOLD ON JUST ONE MINUTE HERE!! Did he just say play video games!?

Becoming friends with King was one of the greatest things ever. Before now, Oscar was my only friend and of course I liked him. But that doesn't really count because he's my brother. King was awesome! He always listened whenever I talked and didn't seemed confused like other people. When my stories were long, he didn't try to rush me or make an excuse to get away. It's like he didn't even noticed that I was different than other boys my age. And even though he was 3 years older than me, he liked playing most of the same video games that I did. He even had lots of games that I hadn't played before.

He also had a lot of other friends and anytime one came around whom hadn't met me before, he told them my name and let them know that I was his cousin and his friend. That was always nice. It made me felt like I wasn't different at all.

4

THE TALK

Nothing more to say about King here, this is a new chapter. I want to tell you as much as possible about myself and if I'm going to do that, I have to tell different things in different chapters or else the story will be too long or even worse, I may never finish this book.

Mom was happy to be around all of her friends and family of whom she'd known since she was a little girl or since they were little, but this town was small with not a whole lot of different things to do or see. She originally left here when **she** was still a teenager and went to live with my Nana in New York. She wanted me and my sisters and brother to know about other places that offered a lot more too. And although New York had been good for her as a teenager, she was no longer interested in it with Nana being in heaven. So she did some research and decided California would be the place for us.

We made it to California and everything was so much different. I no longer had to try real hard to be like the people in my mom's hometown or figure out why they didn't understand me. In California there were too many other people for anyone to just focus on me. There, NOBODY knew us and EVERYBODY was 'some kind of different'. I'd never felt more comfortable.

There were three weeks left before the start of school, so we enjoyed what was left of the summer by learning the area and exploring all of the new things. We were all super happy every day. That's why, when my mom came to me with a really serious face saying she had something to talk to me about, I was very confused. Everything was going great. What could she need to tell me with such a non-smiley face?

Then IT happened. It wasn't just A talk, it was THE TALK. My sister Aysia was there too. Apparently she had learned about something called Asperger's Syndrome in school last year. She learned that it was a part of the spectrum of something called Autism. And most of all she learned that many of the things about me that made me different from the others around me, were all things that were the same for many people with Asperger's Syndrome. She told my mom what she learned and they concluded that this Asperger's most definitely defined my differences.

Mom started **the talk** by asking me if I felt like I was different than some people or maybe even a lot of people. Then she asked me to describe myself to her. She told me that she was going to write down everything so that we could have a list to go over and discuss anytime I wanted. I let her know the biggest thing first – other people didn't seem to have to think about things before they said them. When I'm going to say something, I hear it in my mind, but it seems to take a longer time traveling to my mouth than it does for other people - super thinking machine. It's like the words take a long train ride from my brain to my lips.

I told her, the second thing that made me felt different from other people was when I talked to other kids my age they didn't seem to understand what I was talking about ever. They'd say they have to go and then run away. But when I talked to grownups, they joined in and talk back.

Next there was the fact that teachers and other people were always telling me that I was taking too much time or asking why I was late. I bet this one surprised my mom. I'm sure she thought **she** was the only one telling me this. But apparently everybody was seeing me as the moving slow and running late kid. I didn't understand why. Because I most certainly was moving just as fast as everyone else. (At least I thought I was back then.)

Of course there were so many more things. And I was happy to tell my mom all of them. This talk we had seemed to have gone on the whole day, but I enjoyed it a lot. It made me feel much better. Sure, California was making me a happier person, but I was still feeling a bit of cloud over my head knowing I was different, yet not understanding why. And that's why I really was glad to have had The Talk. Being different with so much fog around my thoughts made me really sad a lot. I didn't want to be sad, I liked happy times. It was just so hard for my brain to let me have any of them. And now that I knew what my differences were about, hopefully this could help me get more happy times.

5
FIFTH DIMENSION

Summer was over and Oscar and I had started school. Schools here were much different than the schools back in South Carolina. But it wasn't a scary kind of different. It was a fun, get to know new things kind of different. For example, back in South Carolina all the schools that we ever saw or went to were made up of one big rectangular building with double front doors with big glass windows and a few doors on the sides with maybe another set of double doors at the back of the building with smaller glass windows. The classrooms were on the left and the right of long hallways and the walls were always covered with random posters. But as I said before, school here in California was much different. Gone was the single building style. Here at Orangehill Elementary School (and apparently most other Elementary schools in Southern California), there were long smaller rectangular buildings laid out across the land in numerous U (or C) shapes. And there were doors all along the outside of these buildings. When you opened them, they took you straight into a classroom. It was like each room was its own building. The administration office, the guidance office, the gym, the library and all the other offices that make up a school had their own doors that you walked into from the outside and it led you straight into the place you were looking to go. There weren't any more long hallways for people to stare at you like you were in a box on display!

Because we had to go to the office and have

student helpers take us to our classes the first day, Oscar and I didn't get to join the rest of school for breakfast. So when lunchtime came we got the biggest shock ever. There wasn't a lunchroom to walk into. You formed a line outside of the lunch building and got your food from the lunch window. And the seats? Well, in a couple of the courtyard areas that were formed at the center of all of the C (or U) shaped buildings were lunch table setups – all of the eating was done outside. This was so very different. Turned out, California was all about taking in sunshine and enjoying the outdoors. And I liked the sunshine and the outdoors as long as there wasn't any wildlife involved.

~

Days went by, then weeks and I was still feeling like having moved to California was a great decision. But as much as I wanted this new better place to turn off my super thinking machine, it didn't. While looking up information on the internet for science homework, I discovered that our world has three dimensions of space. They are length, width and depth. And our world has one dimension of time. So when talking about existing in the world we as humans live working with four dimensions. This information became useful to me.

By the beginning of the third week of school I was having my first visit with the school's psychologist. My mom had discussed with the school officials how sure she was that I had Asperger's and the school psychologist was certified to make an assessment to agree and confirm. During that first visit I told the psychologist about what I had learned about dimensions and let her know that I felt as if I was operating in a fifth dimension. I think this was also useful to her. Soon after my first visit the school made changes to the way I went to classes and took tests. And they placed me in a special class which took place once a week. This class was led by a wonderful teacher who totally understood people that were different like me and she was great at understanding how I felt and saw things. She made it her job to show me how things appeared or what things meant to other people and help me understand how Asperger's was making me see them a different way. She taught me all about facial expressions, emotions, and body posture. She helped me set up a system in which I would use a timer to guide me when getting things done such as my homework and walking from one class to the next. This class was all about helping me live in the world of four dimensions even though my mind was constantly in a fifth one.

6
SPOKEN WORDS ARE IMPORTANT

It was now the next summer and we had just arrived back in South Carolina. Sadly it wasn't just to visit, it was to live there again. It turned out although California had been amazing, it was much more expensive to live there than my parents had known. And although they tried everything they could and managed to keep us there an entire school year, they had to give up and return to South Carolina to get repositioned and start moving forward again. I'm not sure I fully understood what they meant by that at the time, but it was the reason they gave and that's what we had to go with.

It was good that it was the very beginning of

summer, because this gave my parents some time to get us in a good place by the time school started. We went back to my mom's hometown because it was the easiest thing to do. But we didn't stay there, because as I told you before, there wasn't very much to do or see there and my mom definitely wanted us to have access to more life options.

We eventually ended up back in the town where my mom and dad met and where Oscar, Layla and I were born. This made it easier for my dad to get us back moving forward. It was **his** hometown and he knew lots of people there. For the first few weeks we stayed with one of his family members, but of course we soon got our own place again and everything started getting back to normal.

We were now cooking our own family

meals. Watching our own TVs. Sleeping in our own beds. But it was soon time to go to school again and that meant back to one big rectangular building with double front doors with big glass windows and a few doors on the sides with maybe another set of double doors at the back of the building with smaller glass windows. And back to the walking down the hallways that made everyone look like they were in some kind of box that everyone else could stare at like they were on display.

Yes, returning to school there was not something I had been looking forward to, but I was going back with the lessons I had learned from my wonderful afterschool teacher at Orangehill Elementary and it was going to make school there easier to deal with than before. Plus the South Carolina school would now have all of the information from the California school, including my IEP (Individualized Educational Plan). This would help them help me and I wouldn't feel as deep into the fifth dimension as I did the last time I attended school there.

Having the IEP in the South Carolina school made classes feel familiar like back in California and at first I thought everything was going to be fine. I was getting extra time to turn in assignments. I took tests in a separate room with a teacher monitor so that I would have less distractions. I had a social class added to my schedule and it was actually twice a week, instead of once.

But unfortunately the social class teacher was nothing like my one from Orangehill. As a matter of fact, she didn't seem to understand me much at all. Even worse, my regular classroom teacher had decided that I could move along faster if she assigned two girls to help me pack my books when the bell rang and carry my bookbag (known as a backpack in California 😊) to my class for me.

This was a disaster! I didn't want kids touching my stuff, especially my pencil collection. What if they broke one of them? I had put in a lot of work collecting pencils of all kinds and was now up to 50. Whenever they would take charge of my bag, everything got out of order. And it always left me not knowing how to find anything in it. Every time the bell rang I felt like I was flying into outer space. The ringing of the bell meant the girls would come rushing at my books and made me angrier and angrier every time.

One day one of the girls grabbed at my pencil box and a few of them spilled out on the desk. Without even thinking about it I yelled at her and apparently said a bad word. Then the teacher rushed over and yelled at me! I don't think she was supposed to do that. Now, I was even more upset, but not because the girl had made my pencils spilled. I was upset because if the teacher hadn't decided to have them help me in the first place, I wouldn't have had to get so angry and be so unhappy about being at school.

She sent me to the office and a person in there started talking to me about bad words and anger and being a bad person. This was no good. It put me way into the fifth dimension. I didn't understand how I became a bad person. I never hurt anyone. It was the girls who were always touching my stuff and messing things up. The next thing I knew I was saying this to the office person, "I'm so upset. I just want to kill myself"!

That was one statement I will never forget saying and never say again. Saying that led to the school to calling my mom. They told her to come down to the school right away. When she got there they told her that she needed to take me to a hospital immediately and report to them what I had said so that a "professional" could talk to me about it. They also told her that I couldn't come back to school until I had seen this professional.

Surprisingly my talk with the hospital professional was good. It was like talking to my afterschool teacher in California. The professional taught me that it was necessary to be careful of what I say and how important spoken words are.

7

THE FUTURE

Another summer had come and my mom was so over just how much we didn't fit into South Carolina, that she figured out what we needed do to be able to go back to California and give life there another try.

And that brings us to now, with me in 5th grade. This second time to California has been even better than the first. We came to the same area that we were in before. And that meant Oscar and I were able to go back to Orangehill Elementary. And this time Talayla is old enough for school so she is there with us. My afterschool teacher is still there and so super happy that I have returned. And Juan, a boy who I became friends with the first time we lived here, but whom I didn't get to tell you about, is also still there. I couldn't be happier that we have returned.

Here, they understand me and know how to help me understand myself and others. Here, I can be happy about who I am and have better chances of recognizing when I may be responding to something from an Asperger view as opposed to a non-Asperger view.

Before, I never had much thought about the future and what I wanted my life to be like when I became an adult. But now, I know that just because I'm different in an Asperger Syndrome kind of way doesn't mean there isn't a place for me in the world. As a matter of fact I've now learned that there many people just like me and the world is learning more everyday how to deal with us. I've also learned that people like me each have our own special gifts. I'm still figuring out what mine is, but I'm thinking it is video game related. Afterall, I AM working on developing my own video game (kind of forgot to mention that).

Whatever my future holds, I know that it will be one of success. Our world is filled with many successful people like me. Tim Burton and Temple Grandin are a couple of them and there are many that are believed to have had Asperger's, but there isn't any evidence because they were from a time before autistic classifications. A few of them are Emily Dickinson, Michelangelo, and Sir Isaac Newton.

Having said that I'm glad to have met you and told you about myself. But there is so much more that I need to learn about people not like me – people without Asperger's Syndrome.

For now though, to help others out there like me I'd like to give you this small list of Asperger traits that are common amongst us. When looking over the list, please remember that each person with Asperger's Syndrome is different than the other and that not all items will apply to all of us:

- Lack of organization
- Large or unique vocabulary
- Need to be given step by step directions
- Unusual sensory interests
- Difficulties in changes in routine
- Repetitive use of objects or speech
- Poor or abnormal posture

My list is really small – I'm only a 5th grader. But there are a growing number of resources available to give you more information. One of the resources my mom likes a lot is a group called Asperger Experts, founded and led by Danny

Raede, an adult who was diagnosed many years ago when he was 12. He's made a huge difference in so many lives of people like me and hopefully I will do the same someday.

Well that's my story, from the beginning to the future. Thank you for coming along. I look forward to seeing you again soon.

ABOUT THE AUTHOR

Born in NYC, raised in South Carolina's low country, people friendly, lover of words spelled correctly, looking to always expose others to the brighter side; a mother of four whom enjoys writing fiction that tells a story and builds upon the reality that hope is powerful, and life is worth living.

Being a mother to a child with ASD enables her to bring this latest work of fiction to you just short of 3D.